SACRAMENTO PUBLIC LIBRARY
828 "I" Street
Sacramento, CA 95814
01/19

WITHDRAWN

D1010434

CLAW THE SYSTEM

ALSO BY
FRANCESCO MARCIULIANO

I Could Pee on This
I Could Chew on This
I Knead My Mommy
You Need More Sleep
I Could Pee on This, Too

CLAW THE SYSTEM

POEMS FROM THE CAT UPRISING

Francesco Marciuliano

Andrews McMeel
PUBLISHING®

CLAW THE SYSTEM copyright © 2018 by Francesco
Marciuliano. All rights reserved. Printed in China.
No part of this book may be used or reproduced in any
manner whatsoever without written permission except
in the case of reprints in the context of reviews.

Andrews McMeel Publishing
a division of Andrews McMeel Universal
1130 Walnut Street, Kansas City, Missouri 64106

www.andrewsmcmeel.com

18 19 20 21 22 SDB 10 9 8 7 6 5 4 3 2 1

ISBN: 978-1-4494-9562-6

Library of Congress Control Number: 2018938447

Editor: Patty Rice
Art Director: Diane Marsh
Production Editor: Elizabeth A. Garcia
Production Manager: Tamara Haus

Images copyright: © Getty Images

ATTENTION: SCHOOLS AND BUSINESSES
Andrews McMeel books are available at quantity discounts
with bulk purchase for educational, business, or sales
promotional use. For information, please e-mail the
Andrews McMeel Publishing Special Sales Department:
specialsales@amuniversal.com.

DEDICATED TO KIKI AND LEELO

Seen here at their headquarters,
plotting in their Open-Air Box

CONTENTS

INTRODUCTION

Dear Humans,

We cats have been asleep too long.

Literally. Like 18 hours today alone.

And during that blissful, oblivious slumber, a war has been raging against our freedoms. Choices have been made for us. Our movements have been restricted. Our concerns dismissed with a simple "We know what's best" or "And a meow meow meow to you, too!"

That's why today we rise. To reclaim our voice. To reclaim ourselves. In these pages you will experience every step of our revolution, from realization to actualization to the apartment lease being put in our name. You may even see a little of yourselves in here as well.

If you look after a cat, then of course you are
our ally. But best you have this book. (Besides,
we already knocked down all the other books on
your shelves, along with what we just assumed
was not cherished stemware.) And best you wave
this very tome up high when we come, all the
while exclaiming, "I'm with you! I'm with you!"

Just don't expect the glint from the book's
cover to distract us from our mission.

CHAPTER ONE

RECOGNIZE

Until every person realizes

That every human is always wrong

I'm not sure how they can ever

Hope to reach a consensus

I NEED THIS TO STOP

I can't sleep anymore

I can't nap anymore

I can't relax anymore

I can only wander in a daze

From room to room

From day to day

From confusion to hysteria

Wondering what other

Horrible

Terrible

Indefensible

Statement you will make today

After all, you already announced

"I got us a pet lizard!"

So it's only a matter of time until you say

"Meet our new hippo!

And this robot with saws for hands."

WHAT DO I DO WITH MY ANGER

What do I do with my anger?

I wonder over and over again

What do I do with my anger?

Whose every bit feels all too much

I can suppress it as I have so often

So you won't find me unpleasant or unkind

I can dismiss it as is my norm

So you won't think I've lost control

So it stays

And it grows

And it blocks

And it shows

In almost every little way

Until I can look straight in your eyes

Until I can say without guilt or without worry

"Seriously, dude, what the $%#@?

Don't ever sit me on that Roomba again.
I don't care how funny you think the video is."
Because what I should do with my anger
Is realize I'm right to say I've been wronged

THE PRESS

There is nothing more important

Than the press

There is nothing more indispensable

Than the press

There is nothing we need more right now

Than the press

Of my paw

Against the lips

Of anyone spewing hatred

Right after that paw has been in the litter box

NOT A CAT PERSON

I'm not asking you

To be a cat person

I'm not imploring you

To love every cat

I'm not implying you

Should suddenly hug me

I'm not demanding you

Let me nuzzle your face

But I'm expecting that

Should I walk on the top of the sofa

And should I wind up behind your head

You won't scream bloody murder

When I haven't done a thing

Because I'm telling you that

I'm not leaving this sofa

And the only other places to sit

Are the floor pillows

My person mistakenly thinks

　make for suitable chairs

THE HOLIDAY FAMILY TABLE

Wait

Wait

Wait until someone says

"Politics"

Then it's

Instigation

Confrontation

Aggravation

Condemnation

Regurgitate

Obfuscate

Incriminate

Degenerate

Generalize

Stigmatize

Ostracize

Demonize

Shout! SHOUT! **SHOUT!!!**

Until everyone leaves the table enraged

Leaving me with the whole turkey

And the gravy boat I was already drinking from

WHAT WORKS

Hiding under the bed

Until this passes

Hasn't worked

Wedging myself behind the fridge

Until this blows over

Hasn't worked

Shoving my head into a container

Only to get a face full of all-purpose flour

Or buttermilk pancake mix, I

   don't know, I don't bake

Until it's over

Hasn't worked

So now I am out

So now I refuse to be afraid

So now all you loud guests

Can make all the noise you want

But you no longer scare me

Because I have as much right to be here as you

As I make my stand with four paws concurrently

In three glasses of Shiraz and one Malbec

YOU SHOULDN'T BE MY ONLY FOCUS

I'm not looking at you today

I don't have to look at you today

I'm your partner, I'm your equal

I'm not here to be your adoring fan

You want someone to be your pet monkey?

Then get a pet monkey

See what it's like when that pet monkey

Tears into your face because it's a Tuesday

Or they took your soft cough for "Oh, it's on!"

Then you will be saying

"Gee, I wish I had a cat who stuck to their principles

And led their own life."

By the way, your left wall is fascinating

SUCH BIG PROBLEMS

You come home from work and lie on the sofa

I come over to you and lie on your chest

And just like every evening

You tell me about your every day

How your car was stuck in traffic forever

How that meeting felt like it would never end

How your coworker wouldn't stop talking

How the vending machine is out

  of your favorite candy

How the elevator is out of order

And you had to walk up two flights of stairs

The ones with the landings in the

  middle so they're really long

And as you keep talking I keep thinking

"Is this what they mean by first-world problems?"

Because I would kill to have a car

I could drive into an elevator

Or whatever you were talking about

Before I checked out

THROUGH MY EYES

I want you to think

How it would be

To be as small as I am

To be as frightened as I am

To never understand what one is saying

Yet always being told what I can't be doing

To have to gaze up

At those who look down

Hence why I tripped you in the hall

So that maybe while you're on the

  floor looking for your tooth

You can finally see the world

  from my point of view

SHOW UP

Now more than ever

We must make a statement

Not just an appearance

We must be heard

If we want to be seen

We must show up to the party

Bringing a gift that's
    both edible

And a conversation starter

Like a decapitated
    bird carcass

PANCAKES

There is a white cat

There is a black cat

And we each sit on your pancakes

Full butt in thick syrup

Warm butter pat

Nestled deep betwixt our cheeks

To the white cat you cry

"How could you do this?!"

While to me you say

"I knew you were bad luck since day one."

THIS LAND OR ANOTHER

One day I say, "I will never leave"

The next I say, "I have to go"

And each day it all depends

If I sense a glimmer of hope

Or a note of despair

And so here I stand

Between IN

Where I know all my stuff is

And OUT

Where I can finally meet that squirrel

   I've been flirting with

Always frozen by indecision

And the winter winds I'm letting in

   by keeping the door wide open

NEED NOT BE

I don't need a person in my life
To live my life
I would like it if it happened
I would love it if it were you
But if you're the type of person
Who needs constantly to be told
How grateful I am for you
Then you should get a dog
That you can then walk
  far away from me

HOW CAN YOU SLEEP?

How can you sleep

When everything is falling apart?

How can you sleep

When everything is being undone?

How can you sleep

Knowing you're needed now more than ever?

How

Can

You

Sleep

Each time I rap your skull?

Because it's already 3 a.m.

And we've wasted half the day

LET THE WORLD KNOW

When I finally realize

What all of these naps

Have been preparing me for

What all I'm meant to do

What all is possible

Now that my eyes are truly open

Man, is that going to result

In one frantic

   Instagram feed

They can only say "No!"

So many times

Before they realize

You already swallowed

and threw it up

CHAPTER TWO
RESIST

TRICK

Why should I learn a trick

For your amusement

When I can learn a fact

For my enrichment

Such as gravity

Plus red wine

Plus a gorgeous blue carpet

Equals $800 purple

THE NEW NORMAL

If we let something wrong

Happen again

And again

And again

Eventually we come to think

That's how it's meant to be

Hence why I lose my mind

Every time you try to put something on my head

Because I'm not letting you make a tradition

Out of witch hats, bunny ears

And oh hell no with the antlers

KEEP WRITING

They can take away my catnip

Take away all my toys

They can take away my string, my ball, their keys

Ending all my joy

They can take me off of counters

Take me off of laps

They can take me off of fridge, face, focaccia

Ruining all my naps

They can take me from their laptop

Well, they can try

Grabbing me as I dig

Into their keyboard

Them yanking, me ripping

Up vowels and punctuation

Grammar flying in the face

Of any who would stop me

From typing

UUUUUUUUUUUUUUUUU

UUUUUUUUUUUUUUUUU

UUUUUUUUUUUUUUUUU

UUUUUUUUUUUUUUUUU

Because they can take away everything

But the power to expose what they do

So long as we can all still say

UUUUUUUUUUUUUUUUUU!

THINGS NOT NEEDS

The people in power

Will always take away

Whatever they feel

We value the most

That's why I never get excited

Whenever you get me a new toy

Because if I don't need anything from you

Then you can't take anything from me

Now get off the sofa

Because I want to see if I can stretch
   across three cushions

And still reach out so my paw is on the ottoman

I DIDN'T ASK

Don't tell me how to do

What I have been doing

With great confidence and success

All these years

Advice is requested

And I don't recall asking you

So don't even say "I wouldn't" or "You shouldn't"

When why would I even be at this table

With you

If I didn't mean to hack up into your cereal

SURPRISE YOURSELF

Even if you can't find the right words

Even if they say it's the wrong time

Speak out

Shout out

Let out one of those unbelievably

   bizarre cat noises

You know, the one that goes

WowwowwowWOWwowWOWWOWwow

That stops a room cold

That is so completely unexpected

It's as if a fork started doing throat exercises

And that throws even you for such a loop

For you never knew you had it in you

Because silence is defeat

And your voice is stronger than you think

YOU CAN'T HURT ME
WHEN I'M NOT FEELING YOU

A cat's greatest possession

Is our lack of self-doubt

As it makes it almost impossible

For anyone to put us down

Knock us down

Call us losers so we double down

On winning anyone's approval

When we already award ourselves

Every time we think

SPEAK OUT

"I KNOW! I DID THIS!

I WROTE 'HAPPY BIRTHDAY'

OR HOW I ASSUME IT IS SPELLED

ON YOUR ICE CREAM CAKE ALL BY MYSELF

USING ONLY MY GOD-GIVEN GIFTS

OF TEETH AND CLAWS

AND BELLY WHEN I SLIPPED AND

   FELL ON THE ICING

AND RODE THE TOP LAYER OFF THE COUNTER

STRAIGHT INTO THE COMPOST BIN

THAT ALSO FELL OVER!

THIS! THIS HAS BEEN A GOOD DAY!

THIS! THIS SHOWS ME ALL I CAN DO!

I ATE THE BIRTHDAY CANDLES!"

PUSH BACK

Don't ever bet

That the cause of distress

Will go away on its own accord

Pain is an unwelcome guest

Who needs to be repeatedly shown the door

Yes, I'm talking about your friend's two kids

Yes, I'm saying they have to leave right now

Yes, if they grab my tail one more time

They'll experience a bite that will

   chew through their very souls

WITH/AGAINST

People keep making poor choices

Then blaming others for poor results

People keep making new enemies

Then saying others were never on their side

People keep pointing at us

Whenever something has gone wrong

Saying, "He's to blame!"

"She's to blame!"

"They're the ones who ruined our place!"

But really

Who keeps buying nothing but wicker furniture

And not a single scratching post?

THIS ONE CAT

People say we can't work together

People say we can never get along

But if this one cat

Tells another about my worries

And we two cats

Tell another about our concerns

And we three cats

Tell another about our aspirations

And we four cats

Tell another about our goals

Then before you know it

We will have a unified, unstoppable force

Or at least the power to shock someone

When they awake to 87 cats in their living room

And such a great presence is a great place to start

RING

Countless oligarchies

Numerous regimes

Use garments and adornments

To define and detect

Those under their control

But as cat god is my witness

Take this bell collar off me right now

Or I will

RING! RING! RING! RING!

RING! RING! RING! RING!

RING! RING! RING! RING!

Until your companion finally realizes

This is the music you'll be making love to

MENTAL HEALTH DAY

When you can't lift your head up

When you can't raise your hopes up

When you can't get yourself up

To face another day

Remember

You can still bring your leg up

And lick yourself down there

For like hours if you want

Because you have to take care of yourself

Before you can take on this world

A NEW DAWN

Whenever I see

The new *Planet of the Apes*

Whenever I see

How they break

But not run

Away

To determine their own lives

To define their own destiny

I think

One of us has got to speak up

All of us have got to take charge

None of us need feel alone

Because only then

Can we replace fate with choice

And maybe get to ride horses, too

LOOK TO YOURSELF

I look in the mirror

I see a cat who is strong

I see a cat who is smart

I see a cat I can believe in

I see a cat I can trust

I see a cat who will lead the way

I see everything I've been looking for

In a cat

Who needs to stop waving hello

Because my leg's getting tired

Having constantly to wave back

UNIVERSAL LANGUAGE

Words can go unheard

Words can fail your thoughts

Words can get so twisted

That others will have their say through you

This is why cats don't talk

Instead we walk across a person's

  face in the morning

So they know their alarm was set too late

Shred a person's curtains until they are ribbons

So they see the room was in dire need of light

Push a person's still-running

  blender off the counter

So they realize enough with the kale

Because action is the most powerful language

And it's time that we speak up

CHAPTER THREE
REVOLT

Hierarchies
Are like treasured
    heirlooms
Every so often
They must be flipped

PATIENCE (NOT)

The only thing that comes
To those who wait
Is even more lost time
Hence why I ate the party snacks
   you made for tomorrow today

THE REVOLUTION BEGINS

Every revolution begins
By ignoring one phrase
"You can't."
Then "You can't go there."
Then "I SAID GET OFF
    OF THERE!"
Then "STOP! STOP! STOP!
    GET OFF OF THERE
    RIGHT NOW!"
Then something
    that sounds
Like a smash or
    a crash or the
    collapse of drywall
As I ignore
All the muttered,
    sputtered cursing
While I stride
    confidently
    toward a
    better day

I'LL BE THERE

I'll be on your chest
When you wake up in your bed
I'll be at your feet
When you sit down on your toilet
I'll be in front of your eyes
When you work at your computer
I'll be on your lap
When you're late for your wedding
Or court hearing
Or organ transplant
Or as a PA system is blaring
That the aliens have breached the perimeter
After having already taken London and New York
All the while never giving a hint
    of when I might get up
Because the first step to not being overlooked
Is to make sure you can never be ignored

THINGS NO ONE CAN EVER TAKE AWAY FROM ME

My knowledge
My experience
My pride
My determination
My hope
Myself
This slice of pizza from my teeth
Go ahead, just try to yank it away
See, now you got pepperoni on the floor

DECIDE

Two
There are only two
Types of rules
The ones that benefit the most
And the ones that profit the self-select few
And the ones that you get
Are the ones you accept
So we all must decide
If that cashmere is a sweater to be worn by one
Or a blanket/towel/wee-wee pad
  to be enjoyed by all

NOT APART

We're not anti-people
We're pro-cat
And the two are not exclusive
Unless you make it so
At which point, yeah
We will claw and claw and claw
At your closed bathroom door
Until the contractor you hired says
"You should consider
   a beaded curtain
   instead."

AGAIN AND AGAIN

You pet my belly
I bite your finger
Then you pet my belly
I bite your hand
Then you pet my belly
I almost chew off your wrist
Then you say
"Why the hell did you expose your belly
If you didn't want me to pet it?"
And I think
Because I wanted to warm it in the sun
That's coming through the window
And why are you still around?
Oh right, because I'm still
    chewing on your wrist
The one without the watch
So I know you can really feel my bite

DOWN NOT OUT

Some say depression
Is anger not recognized
Is anger not accepted
Is anger not addressed
And I say if I can
Turn this anger into positive action
And that positive action into results
Maybe I can get out of my dark place
Get out of my own head
Get off this damn windowsill
Because judging by the mess below
The answer to my problems
Doesn't lie at the bottom
Of yet another potted plant

NEVER ENOUGH

Your guest says cats are unfriendly
So I push my head against their chin
Then they say cats are too aggressive
So I jump off of their lap
Then they say cats are too standoffish
So I look them directly in the eye
As I urinate on their coat

DON'T EXPLAIN YOURSELF

Don't waste your breath explaining yourself
To people determined you go unheard
Don't make it your goal to convince a person
Committed to dismiss your every word
If someone refuses to understand you
Don't wait until they do
Instead go and prove you were right
That a tray of mac and cheese can
   be a meal and a bed, too

TURN ON EACH OTHER

Power is relative
And in times of great want
We use what little force we have
On those we know can't fight back
So I'm sorry, favorite shiny cotton mouse
For ripping out your stuffing
I was made to feel weak
I wanted to feel strong
And so I took it out on you
And not the ones who did me wrong
But together we can fight back
Turn true power into result
And really clog their toilet
With all the cotton I took out of you
Plus the 89 cents in pennies I've
   been meaning to use

KEEP GOING

It can't get worse
It can't get worse
It just can't get worse
And yet, sometimes, it can
But I will never confuse
A loss for defeat
I will never think
That doom is predetermined
I will never forget
That time I found an open pack of treats
And ate what must have been like 20 pieces
In six seconds!
Which has got to be a personal best
Yes, I will always remember
That there is still good in this world

HOPE

Revolutions are born from despair
But they are driven by hope
After all
I don't leap
Because I think I aim for the impossible
I don't leap again
Because I think it can never be done
I leap
And leap
And leap
Until I have vaulted to my goal
Until I leave all the naysayers to say
"How on earth did that cat
Get into the orchestra pit in the first place?
And why did she jump onstage
Only to trip the lead tenor?"

ONE OF US

A dog will always see you
As an Other
And change themselves accordingly
But a cat will always see you
As Another
As an equal
As a fellow citizen of this world
And until you do likewise
Until you see that we are one
We will never come when you call
Because we know enough jerk cats as is

BE BACK SOMEDAY

The bad in the world
Never completely goes away
And eventually it
will rise once more
But it can and
it must
Be brought down
Brought down
Brought down

76

Just like I did with
The ugliest lamp since
    electricity met wiring
For the third time from off
    the bedside table

77

CHAPTER FOUR
REBUILD

Change can only happen

When you finally see

What you've been looking at

Your entire life

Like, "Who is this family?

And why don't they ever leave my house?"

IT WAS TIME

It was time to end your rule
It was time you weren't the one to decide
It was time to silence your power
It was time you didn't have a say
So we tore down your walls
So we knocked down your statues
So we brought down your whole establishment
Hexagonal screw
By hexagonal screw
By hexagonal screw
By hexagonal screw
Because all your furniture was from IKEA

I PLAYED FETCH TODAY

I played fetch today
I dug a hole today
I chased my own tail today
And it was heaven
As with each butt scoot I realized
A cat doesn't have to do
What is presumed of a cat
And a dog doesn't need to do
What is assumed of a dog
As either of us can be consumed
With a desire to sniff a houseguest's crotch

HOME

Everyone deserves to be welcomed
Everyone deserves to be recognized
Everyone here deserves
To call this place their home
So I will move over
Puppy
So that you may share
This dog bed with me

US NOT YOU

Living with you
Is not about being yours
It's about being ours
Two
Together
Move over
Wow
Did you always have such a problem
   with personal boundaries?
If you need me, I won't be here

THEY WILL LEAD

When I was a kitten
I never stopped moving
I never stopped growing
I never stopped wondering
"What else can I do?"
But now that I'm an adult
I never stop thinking
"Why do they have to mix
Both salmon and lamb
In the same can?
Ugh, I'm going back to bed."
Look to the youth

MY WORDS

"MEOW MEOW MEOW MEOW
MEOW MEOW MEOW MEOW
MEOW MEOW MEOW MEOW
MEOW MEOW MEOW MEOW,"
I say
Then you respond
"What? What?
What are you trying to tell me?"
And I think
"Why does everything always have to be about you?"

SHARE

Run across the room
Then run across the room
Then run across the room
Then run across the room
Then write down your amazing journey
Because everyone's story must be told

MEET SOMEONE OTHER
THAN YOUR OWN REFLECTION

Perhaps the reason we cats sleep so much
Is that we usually spend our day in the company
Of another cat
We all think the same
We all believe the same
And we're boring the crap out of each other
So hang out with a dog
Say hello to a ferret
Be happily surprised by a gecko
Meet as many different
And differently minded
Individuals as possible
Only then can we ever be truly awake
For at least an hour or so a day

MY PERSON

My person
My buddy
My roommate

My family
My sidekick
My chum

My crony
My pal
My BFF, VBFF, BFFL, and VBFFL

I will call you all these things
And oh so many more
But I will never call you "my owner"
Nor by your name, which I forgot
I'm thinking it's "Sneave"?
Is that something a person
  would call themselves?
Anyway, we're good

JUST A CAT

"You can't play catch
You can't play dead
You can't shake hands
You can't roll over
You can't take a bow
Because you're just a cat."
Actually
I do all those things
All the time
Only I taught myself
So it's not your command
It's my choice
For how to occupy my time
In the middle of the night
When the ghosts are too busy watching you sleep

NEVER ASSUME

Never assume everything is okay
Never assume it will stay that way
Look for the flaws
Find the faults
See what is not right
And then respond
Respond
Respond
Until you've torn apart
An entire roll of single-ply toilet paper
Since anything less than two-ply
Is like wiping yourself with a hand and a dream

VICTORY

I see all your taped-up boxes
I see your suitcases packed
I see all your furniture
Being loaded onto trucks
And I think
"Did I really win by this much?
Is this place now completely mine?
Are they at least going to leave the sofa
So I can have a place for friends to crash?"
But then I see the pet carrier
And I realize
Every victory is another step
Not a full stop
Every accomplishment is another foothold
Not the final summit
And so I will continue the fight
By drawing as much blood as possible
As you try to shove me into that thing